Erik Erikson: Post-Freudian Theory

Erik Erikson: Post-Freudian Theory
Steven G. Carley MS

N Charleston

Steven grows-up in a small town in Boston, Massachusetts playing with other children in his neighborhood. Steven leads a mostly quiet life spending much of his time devoted to his studies. Steven views himself more as a curious person than as a genius. He was born on July 13, 1975, his father was a machinist and mother Beverly was daughter to a machinist. Steven liked running and climbing but most of all he liked collecting, match box cars, baseball cards, muscle men figures, and pretty much anything else he could get his hands on. Steven grows-up with his two sisters who as mentioned earlier lead a relatively quiet life.

Steven at times rebels at home by sneaking out of the house at night to join in the endeavors of locals in the neighborhood. Steven succeeds within University of Phoenix receiving a Bachelor of Science degree graduating with honors. Steven has written 40 total in print books. This is where most of Steven's authority in writing resides. Through his intense study and writing routine he has become an SME in various domains. He is currently continuing his studies within a terminal master's degree IO psychology program at SNHU of which he is being conferred during the summer of 2015.

stevecarley.us

Contents

Erik Erikson: Post-Freudian Theory

Erik Erikson, the man who single handedly coined the phrase identity crisis. Erikson's world fame in multiple fields includes education, psychohistory, anthropology, and psychoanalysis, all without a college degree of any kind. Erikson extends the assumptions of Freud unlike other theorists who repudiate Freud's findings offering a novel outlook in the process (Erikson, 1963). The post-Freudian theory of Erik Erikson acts as an extension to the infantile developmental stages of Freud incorporating stages of adolescence, adulthood, and old age. The suggestion of Erikson is that contributing to the formation of personality is a psychosocial struggle during each stage. This struggle takes the form of an identity crisis from adolescence on, acting as a turning point in one's life that can either weaken or strengthen one's personality. Erikson's post-Freudian theory is an extension of psychoanalysis, one that Erikson believes that in time Freud himself may have covered. Although Erikson's lifecycle approach to personality makes use of Freudian theory as the foundation, several differences exist between Freud and Erikson. Erikson places more emphasis on both historical and social influences in addition to his elaboration of psychosexual stages beyond childhood. Like those of other personality theorists, Erik Erikson's post-Freudian theory is a reflection of his personal background including a lifelong search for his identity, experiences with a variety of cultures, extensive travels, and the arts.

Erik Erikson: Post-Freudian Theory

ISBN-13: 978-1514265567
ISBN-10: 1514265567

DEDICATION

This book is dedicated to anyone assisting in its creation. To all those who wish for my success and benefit from the book's success. It is my hope that my work can be compared to other literature and recognized for the time and precision in its completion.

Erik Erikson: Post-Freudian Theory
Steven G Carley MS

Print Edition

Biography of Erik Erikson

Erik Salomonsen as a child wonders who his biological father to be. The identity of his mother is of no secret as she was a splendidly beautiful Danish/Jewish woman whose family often stress their Danish roots. The young boy holds three separate beliefs of his origins having been born into a single parent family. His first belief is for the husband to his mother Theodor Homburger, a physician, was his father. The maturing Erik grew to realize his blonde hair and blue eyed features not to match the dark features of Homburger or his mother. The boy wanted answers so his mother gave him one, a lie stating her first husband Valdemar Salomonsen had abandoned her when she was pregnant and that this man to be his biological father. The bright young lad Erik was did not believe this story for a second because he knew Salomonsen had left his mother four years before he was even born. Erik grew to believe through a fair-minded deduction for him to be the product of a sexual liaison between an aristocratic artistically gifted Dane and his mother. This is the story for Erik to believe for the majority of his life. While seeking the name of his biological father, Erik also searches for his own identity.

The Scandinavian features of Erik contribute to his identity confusion during his school days. His blue eyes and blonde hair gave him the appearance of an outsider when he attended temple. He was referred to as a Jew by his Aryan classmates while in public school making Erik feel out of place in both arenas. Eric had difficulty throughout his life accepting himself as either Gentile or Jew. At the age of 58, Erik loses his mother and a fear grows in Erik of never knowing the true identity of his biological father. Erik eventually loses interest in finding the identity of his true father nearly 30 years later with the deterioration of his mind and body. Erik continues to demonstrate identity confusion. As an example, Erik rarely speaks in English despite it being his primary language for 60 years. He decides instead to speak in his native tongue in German. Erik long-held an affinity for Denmark, although never living there and took pride in displaying the flag of Denmark.

Questions arise of who was Erik Erikson the man. Was he a Gentile or Jew? Was he an American, German, or Dane? Was he a psychoanalyst or artist? Even Erikson seemed to not have the answers to such questions, spending the entirety of his life determining his very own identity. During late adolescence, Erikson ventures far from home to discover his niche in life, adopting the lifestyle of a wandering poet and artist. After nearly seven years of searching and drifting, Erikson returns home exhausted, depressed, confused, and unable to paint or sketch. A fortuitous event changes Erikson's life at this time. Erikson's friend Peter Blos sends him a letter with an invitation to teach children at a Viennese school. Anna Freud is one of the school's founders who acts as not only his employer but also psychotherapist. While receiving treatment from Anna Freud, Erikson divulges his concern of finding the true identity of his father. Ms. Freud gives Erikson little empathy, telling him to stop fantasizing about his unknown father. Erikson could not take Ms. Freud's advice to give-up his search to find his father's identity, although he seldom if ever did not take the advice given by Anna Freud.

Erikson meets Joan Serson in Vienna, and with Anna Freud's permission he marries the Canadian born teacher, artist, and dancer who also receives psychoanalysis from

Anna Freud. With Joan's facility in the English language and her background in psychoanalysis, she becomes a valuable coauthor and editor of Erikson's books. Erikson is taken through some difficult experiences in his search for identity during his development in the adulthood stage. This stage according to Erikson has the requirement of an individual to take care of ideas, products, and children that he or she generate. Erikson was deficient on this issue in meeting his own standards. His son Neil was born with Down Syndrome, and Erikson did not take good care of him. Erik agreed to place Neil in an institution while Joan was still under sedation at the hospital. When they went home, Erikson told his three other children that their brother died at birth. He lied to them as his mother had lied to him of the true identity of his father. His oldest son Kai was given the truth but he continued to lie to his two other children. The distress his mother's lie to bring Erikson, he does not consider the stress his children may bear with the lie he casts on them. Erikson violates two of his own principles by lying to his children, don't pit family members against each other and don't lie to people you should care for. When Neil dies around the age of 20 to compound the situation, the Erikson's who were away at Europe request of Jon and Sue to handle the funeral arrangements for a brother they never knew existed (Friedman, 1999). The identity of Erikson was also sought through the myriad changes of places of residence and jobs. Erikson had no specific professional identity lacking any academic credentials and was variously known as a public intellectual, a psychobiographer, critic, existentialist, cultural anthropologist, professor, clinician, psychoanalyst, psychologist, and artist.

Erik and his family leave Vienna for Denmark in 1933 with fascism on the rise in an effort to gain Danish citizenship.

Erikson ends-up leaving Copenhagen and immigrating to the United States after Danish officials refuse his request. Erikson's name changes from Homburger to Erikson in the United States. This change represents a retreat from his earlier Jewish identification and was a crucial turning point in his life. Erikson resented this implication that his name change was an abandonment from his Jewish heritage. These charges were countered by Erikson who points-out the use of his full name in his essays and books Erik Homburger Erikson. In time, Erikson drops his middle name on his books, replacing it with the initial H. Hence, the person who became known as Erik H. Erikson had previously been known as Erik Homburger Erikson, Erik Homburger, and Erik Salomonsen. Erikson's pattern of moving from place to place continues in America. Erikson sets up a modified psychoanalytic practice while in Boston. He accepts research positions at Harvard Psychological Clinic, Harvard Medical School, and Massachusetts General Hospital without any kind of college degree nor medical credentials.

Erikson takes a position at Yale in 1936, wanting to write but not having the time while in Boston and Cambridge. He moves to University of California, Berkeley after 2.5 years but not long before his move to South Dakota to study the Pine Ridge Reservation and the people of the Sioux Nation. Later he lives in northern California with the people of the Yurok Nation, and these experiences in cultural anthropology add to the completeness and richness of his concept of humanity. Erikson gradually evolves a theory of personality during his California period compatible but separate from Freud's. Erikson publishes Childhood and Society in 1950, a somewhat hodgepodge of unrelated chapters at first glance. Erikson originally encounters difficulty in finding a common theme underlying such topics as Hitler's childhood, the eight stages of human development, the growth of the ego, and childhood in two Native American tribes. Erikson eventually comes to the realization, however, that the influence of historical, cultural, and psychological factors on identity is the element binding the chapters together. The classic Childhood and Society becomes gives Erikson a reputation as an imaginative thinker and is a fine introduction to his post-Freudian theory of personality.

The officials at University of California demand a pledge of loyalty to the United States requesting its faculty members in 1949 to sign an oath. This was not uncommon of the times when the belief as urged by Senator Joseph McCarthy is that Communism is poised to take over the government. Erikson refuses to sign the oath despite not being a Communist. The recommendation of the Committee on Privilege and Tenure was for Erikson to retain his position, yet he leaves California for Massachusetts working at Austen Riggs as a therapist, a treatment center for psychoanalytic research and training in Stockbridge. He returns to Harvard in 1960 and holds the position of professor of human development for the next 10 years. Erikson continues an active career after retirement seeing a few patients, lecturing, and writing. He lives in Marin County, California during the early years of his retirement, Cape Cod, and Cambridge, Massachusetts. Erikson continues to seek his father's name through all these changes. At the age of 91, Erikson passes away on May 12, 1994.

The answer to who was Erik Erikson may be one at which even Erikson himself may not have a conclusive response. Through the brilliantly constructed books, lectures, and essays, one can learn much about the man known as Erik

Erikson. The best known works of Erikson include A Way of Looking at Things (1987), The Lifecycle Completed (1982), Identity and the Lifecycle (1980), Life History and the Historical Moment (1975), Dimensions of a New Identity (1974), Ghandi's Truth (1969), Identity: Youth and Crisi (1968), Young Man Luther (1958), and Childhood and Society (1950, 1963, 1985).

Post-Freudian Theory

Post-Freudian theory is a product of Erik Erikson. Despite Erikson's lack of formal training, he successfully contributes to Freud's developmental stages of infancy incorporating an adolescent stage, adulthood stage, and a developmental stage of old age. Erikson's developmental stages focus on psychosocial development contributing to personality. From the time of adolescence is an identity crisis which can strengthen or weaken the personality. Erikson considers his theory to be an extension of Freudian theory. Similar to Freud, Erikson takes a life cycle approach to personality yet differs from Freud in many respects. Erikson creates a more in-depth description of the developmental stages beyond childhood and places more emphasis on historical and social influences.

Erikson finds the ego to be a positive force helping to shape the self-identity. The ego represents the center of the personality, allowing for reactions to conflict which maintain individuality despite the forces of society. Childhood is a time when the ego remains fragile yet during adolescence will begin to gain strength. Throughout the stages of development the ego will unify personality. To Erikson, the ego represents an unconscious entity organizing present experiences with past versions of self and anticipations of self. Erikson's definition of the term ego is individual ability to unify the self and adapt to experiences (Erikson, 1963). Erikson identifies three aspects of ego: the body ego, the ego ideal, and ego identity. The body ego makes reference to bodily experiences and presents a method of viewing physical attributes as different than those of another. The ego ideal is representative of self-image in comparison with an established ideal. The responsibility of the ego ideal is the satisfaction of the physical self and personal identity. Self-image within the various social roles refers as the ego identity. These three components body ego, ego ideal, and ego identity alter throughout the developmental stages yet most abruptly during adolescence. The emergence and shaping of the ego is a result of societal influence. The ego develops its potential at birth, yet must emerge as a product of the environment. Societies show variations in child rearing practices, shaping personalities to fit the values of culture. One of Erikson's contributions to personality theory is his extension of the developmental stages to include school age to old age. Erikson's belief ego development is an occurrence throughout the developmental stages is in accordance with an epigenetic principle, implying a step by step growth of fetal organs. The ego too can follow an epigenetic principle with each stage of development occurring at a proper time. Stages do not replace each other yet emerge from the previous stage. Egoistic epigenetic development follows the same path as physical development as an infant must first learn to crawl before he or she can walk. While they are crawling, they develop the potential to perform more complex tasks and even when these complex tasks are realized they continue to demonstrate the ability to perform less complex tasks (Erikson, 1963). The epigenetic principle represents the first three Eriksonian stages: infancy, early childhood, and play age (Erikson, 1968; Erikson, 1982).

Erikson's stages of psychosocial development follow some basic assumptions. The eight stages of Erikson's psychosocial development take place in accordance to the epigenetic principle, stating the stages do not replace each other yet emerge from previous stages. During each stage of life is an interaction of opposites incorporating a conflict between syntonic (positive) and dystonic (negative) elements. This can be seen within the interaction during infancy of basic trust and basic mistrust. An infant must learn mistrust to not remain unprepared to the realities of the world and must learn trust to not be cynical or suspicious. The conflict between syntonic and dystonic elements continues throughout the developmental stages producing either ego quality or ego strength referred as according to Erikson basic strength. Through the arguments made in direct contrast of another hope emerges from trust and mistrust allowing an infant to move to the next stage of life. If during a stage the clash between syntonic and dystonic elements is minimal, the result can be core pathology resulting in hopelessness. Erikson's stages although described as psychosocial continue to consist of a biological aspect to development. The occurrence of events during earlier stages of development do not result in personality development during later stages. The conflicts and events shaping ego identity are past, present, and future. An identity crisis is present during each stage but especially so during and after adolescence. This time is a turning point exposing both vulnerabilities and potentials. With the emergence of a crisis, the self-identity becomes susceptible to modification. An identity crisis is not necessarily a disaster, yet an opportunity for adjustment either adaptive or maladaptive (Erikson, 1968).

Within Erikson's eight stages of psychosocial development basic strengths emerge from the syntonic and dystonic elements typifying each stage. Each stage consists of an antithetical as well as complementary relationship. The basic strength during infancy is hope and the syntonic and dystonic elements are basic trust versus basic mistrust. The basic strength during early childhood is will and the syntonic and dystonic elements are autonomy versus shame and doubt. The basic strength during play age is purpose and the syntonic and dystonic elements are initiative versus guilt. The basic strength during school age is competence and the syntonic and dystonic elements are industry versus inferiority. The basic strength during adolescence is fidelity and the syntonic and dystonic elements are identity versus identity confusion. The basic strength during young adulthood is love and the syntonic and dystonic elements are intimacy versus isolation. The basic strength during adulthood is care and the syntonic and dystonic elements are generativity versus stagnation. The basic strength during old age is wisdom and the syntonic and dystonic elements are integrity versus despair and disgust (Erikson, 1982).

The most significant interpersonal relationship during infancy is with one's mother or caregiver. Basic trust is learned when the infant learns the mother will provide food on a regular basis. Basic trust can be increased with a comforting voice and exciting visual environment. Basic mistrust can be learned when physiological needs and environmental needs are not met. Basic trust is syntonic and basic mistrust dystonic as infants must develop both attitudes to not become gullible or hostile during later stages of development. Infants at one time or another will experience trust and mistrust through feedings and frustration. It is critical to consist of a ratio of both trust and mistrust to adapt and be weary of danger. Trust versus mistrust is the first psychosocial crisis and those who solve this crisis achieve hope. Hope develops from the first syntonic and dystonic elements of basic trust and mistrust. Through the painful and pleasurable experiences of infancy, infants will learn and develop expectations for distress and satisfaction. If infants do not develop hope, they will experience withdrawal resulting in future psychological disturbance.

Erikson's second psychosocial stage of development is early childhood encompassing the second and third years of life. Pleasure during early childhood involves mastery of bodily functions. Children will develop self-control over themselves as well as demonstrate control over their interpersonal environment. Childhood is a time of experiencing doubt and shame in an attempt at acquiring autonomy and the acquisition of will. Psychosexual development during the second year of life goes through an anal urethral muscular mode. Children learn mobility and control their bodies to remain cleanly. Early childhood is a time of toilet training as well as learning to walk, run, and play. Children may display stubbornness through retention and elimination of feces or snuggling and pushing away mother as well as hoard objects to then ruthlessly discard them. Early childhood is a time of contradiction of a loving cooperative child who at the same time is hateful and resistant. This contradiction is the result of the conflict of autonomy versus shame and doubt (Erikson, 1968). Early childhood can be seen as a time of autonomy and shame and doubt. A child's stubborn expression can result in an inhibited view of culture.

Parents may shame their children for poor behavior and doubt their abilities at the same time to meet such standards. The psychological crisis of early childhood is autonomy versus shame and doubt. Children should develop a ratio of autonomy and shame and doubt consisting of more autonomy. Development of too little autonomy can result in a lack of basic strengths during later stages of development. Autonomy grows from basic trust without which a child will be met with shame and doubt and a serious psychosocial crisis. Shame and doubt is a feeling of self-consciousness and uncertainty which remains hidden. The dystonic qualities of shame and doubt grow from basic mistrust. A resolution of the crisis between autonomy versus shame and doubt results in the basic strength of will. This is the beginning of will power yet the measure of free will occurs during later stages of development. The child's conflict is their quest for autonomy and the parent's exhibition of control using shame and doubt. The development of will within children is dependent on environmental allowance of bodily expression. An excess of shame and doubt will result in the failure to attain the basic strength of early childhood. Without the development of will is the presence of compulsion resulting in lack of purpose and lack of confidence during the subsequent stages of development.

Erikson's third stage of development refers as the play age spanning from approximately the ages of three to five. Genital locomotor is the primary psychosexual mode during the play age. Erikson views the Oedipus complex as childhood imagination and an introduction to reproduction, future, and death. A girl may envy boys because of social contingencies and a boy's anxiety of threats of loss references parts of the body. The Oedipus complex produces no harmful effects on later personality development unless subject to the provocation of social sex play or sexual abuse (Erikson, 1963). Childhood interest in genital activity is a product of moving from place to place. Children can now run and jump and their play becomes imaginative. The development of will during the preceding stage is building a sense of purpose in a child's life. Childhood cognition incorporates imagery of the grown-up self, which can at times produce guilt contributing to the psychosocial crisis during the play age initiative versus guilt. Children can now move more freely as genital interest stirs, they begin to approach the world in a goal-oriented fashion. Their initiative at the same time must be abandoned as they must repress goals to marry mother or father. Such repression stirs guilt, the dystonic element of the psychosocial crisis initiative versus guilt. The ratio between the two should favor initiative, although openly expressed initiative can lead to chaos and a deficiency of morality in regard to principle. Dominance of the dystonic element guilt can result in inhibitions constituting play age pathology. The basic strength of the play age is purpose as children play to win as mother and father tend to be objects of sexual desire. Goals are pursued purposively as the conscience develops concurrently acting as the cornerstone of morality (Erikson, 1968).

School age spans the ages of approximately six to thirteen. The social world no longer is limited to only family and expands to include peers and other adult role models. The child's quest for confidence involves a strong desire to attain knowledge. Children diligently strive to attain the skills required of their culture. Whereas all cultures do not use schools to instruct children, the term school age does not pertain exclusively to schooling. This is only to say this is a time of instruction of the skills needed to be a competent member of society. Psychosexual latency occurs during the school age as children are more concerned with learning technology and strategies of interacting socially. Through work and play, children begin to view themselves as competent or incompetent. These self-images of competency are the origin of the ego identity. School age is a time of tremendous social growth the psychosocial crisis of which is industry versus inferiority. Industry references one's ability to remain busy and complete a task. School age learning gears toward activities of the acquisition of job skills and rules of cooperation. Children who learn and perform well develop a sense of industry, yet failure to accomplish goals results in the dystonic element of inferiority. Inadequacies of previous stages of development can contribute to feelings of inferiority. Failure is not inevitable should one not attain the syntonic elements of previous stages. The ratio of industry and inferiority as with other stages should consist of a majority of the syntonic element yet should consist of some dystonic qualities. Inferiority can act as motivation to do one's best, yet an abundance of inferiority can result in feelings of incompetence. The psychosocial conflict of school age is industry versus inferiority which develops into the basic strength of competence. This competence is a confidence in one's physiological and cognitive ability to successfully perform school age tasks. Competence is the gateway to cooperation and a productive adult life (Erikson, 1968). A psychosocial crisis favoring either inferiority or an abundance of industry can result in regression to earlier stages of development. The result is infantile fantasy and nonproductive play. The term for such a regression is inertia opposing competence as the core of school age pathology.

Adolescence composes of the time from puberty to adulthood and is a crucial developmental stage requiring the acquisition of a sense of ego identity. Adolescence is neither the beginning nor end of the ego identity, yet is most crucial during the psychosocial conflict of identity versus identity diffusion. The emergence from this crisis is the basic strength of fidelity. As Erikson views school age as sexual latency, he views adolescence as social latency. Adolescents are rewarded the luxury of postponing commitments, especially within the western society while establishing their ego identity. To Erikson puberty plays a minor role in adolescence presenting no sexual crisis. Puberty is important psychologically triggering the expectations of social roles assisting in the struggle for ego identity. The adolescent search for who they are and ego identity reaches its climax during adolescence. Adolescents search for new roles drawing from the acceptance and rejection of earlier self-images. Identity develops during earlier stages and becomes a crisis during adolescence, the struggle between identity and identity diffusion. A crisis should not be viewed as a catastrophe yet as a turning point lasting for years resulting in increased or decreased ego strength (Erikson, 1968). The emergence of identity according to Erikson consists of two sources adolescent affirmation of childhood identification and the social context encouraging conformity to societal standards (Erikson, 1982). Adolescents often turn the values of their peers as a measure of standard as identity is shaped substantially by society. Identity can be both positive and negative, as adolescents decide what they do and do not want to become. At times, they must disapprove of parental and peer values intensifying identity confusion. Identity confusion involves a division of self-image, inability to establish intimacy, and a rejection of standards of family and community. Just as the other stages require some dystonic element, so too does adolescence require identity confusion. Part of the evolution of identity stability is the experience of doubt and confusion of one's self-image. This can involve gang membership and experimentation with drugs and sex or the quiet ponderance of where one fits in the world. Identity confusion though necessary can lead to regression to earlier stages of development in abundance. Adolescents avoid adult responsibility drifting from one sexual relationship to another, one job to another, and one set of ideas to another. Development of the correct ratio of identity to identity confusion results in faith in motivational principles, free choice toward behavior, trust in advice regarding goals, and confidence in choice of occupation. One will emerge with the basic strength of fidelity should he or she conquer the adolescent psychosocial crisis. With establishment of standards of conduct, adolescents are no longer in need of parental guidance. Trust learned during adolescence assists in the establishment of fidelity during adolescence. Faith in the future is dependent on trust and hope as well as the other basic strengths of will, purpose, and competence. Should one not attain fidelity, he or she may suffer the core pathology of adolescence role repudiation, blocking the synthesis of self-image and values. Role repudiation involves an extreme lack of self-confidence expressed through shyness or rebellion toward authority. Some role repudiation can help an adolescent to evolve their personal identity and injects vitality into the social structure (Erikson, 1982).

Young adulthood occurs between the ages of 19 and 30, focusing on the acquisition of intimacy and development of generativity. Young adults experience the conflict of intimacy versus isolation in the attempt of acquiring the basic strength of love. Sexual relations during adolescence are self-serving in the search for identity. Genitality, the components of sexuality, develops during young adulthood distinguished by trust and sexual satisfaction with a loved person existing only within an intimate relationship (Erikson, 1963). The psychosocial crisis during young adulthood is intimacy versus isolation. Intimacy is the fusion of one's identity with another without fear of losing identity. The achievement of intimacy is dependent on the formation of a stable ego. Uncertainty in one's ego can cause one to either shy away from or desperately seek intimacy through meaningless sexual encounters. Intimacy in its mature form is an ability to share trust and demonstrate compromise. Marriage should require intimacy yet many marry as a search for identity from a failure to establish during adolescence. The dystonic element of young adulthood is isolation or the absence of true intimacy (Erikson, 1968). Financial and social success is not a criteria determining isolation when one does not attend to the responsibilities of procreation and mature love. To acquire mature love, one should have some degree of isolation as an abundance of togetherness can diminish ego identity leading to regression and an inability to face adulthood. Even too much togetherness is not as great a danger as too much isolation and too little intimacy, making it difficult to attain the basic strength during young adulthood of love emerging from the psychosocial crisis of intimacy versus isolation. Love involves intimacy and a degree of isolation, permitting each partner to retain a separate identity. Mature love requires commitment, passion, and friendship and as the basic strength of young adulthood enables one to be productive during adulthood and old age. The core pathology of young adulthood is exclusivity which in small amounts is necessary to attain intimacy. The reason is people must demonstrate the ability to exclude people and ideas to develop a sense of identity. When one's ability to cooperate is blocked exclusivity becomes pathological.

Erikson's seventh stage of psychosocial development is adulthood when people begin to take their place in society and even assume responsibility for the production of society. This stage of development is the longest spanning the years of 31 to 60. The psychosexual mode of procreativity characterizes adulthood. The psychosocial crisis occurring during adulthood is generativity versus stagnation as the battle to attain the basic strength of care. Erikson's psychosexual theory makes the assumption an instinctual drive perpetuates the species. The drive is similar to the instinct to procreate and is an extension of young adulthood genitality (Erikson, 1982). Procreativity references more than just genital contact, making the assumption of responsibility to care for offspring. Procreation should follow intimacy and love established during young adulthood. Mature adults want more than sexual contact, they want commitment to raising offspring. The syntonic element of adulthood is generativity marking a new generation with new ideas. Generativity concerns itself with guiding the next generation through work, procreating children, and contributing to the world. People have an altruistic need to instruct not only one's own children but also to other young people. Generativity grows from intimacy and identity. Adults seek more than one on one intimacy as the need to instruct others in the ways of society emerges. This motivation to instruct others is not selfish yet an evolutionary drive to contribute to the younger generations to better ensure the continuation of human society. The dystonic element of adulthood is self-absorption and stagnation. When people become self-absorbed, the generative cycle of productivity falters. This self-indulgence fosters stagnation, yet as in other stages a ratio of the dystonic element is necessary to attain the basic strength in this case care. Care to Erikson is a widening of commitment to care for others and products (Erikson, 1982). Care arises from the basic strengths of previous stages. To care for that which one cares for, he or she must consist of all of the basic strengths from the previous stages. Care is not an obligation yet a desire to emerge from the conflict of generativity versus stagnation. The core pathology of adulthood is rejectivity which is an unwillingness to care for others. Rejectivity is a result of self-centeredness and a feeling others are inferior. Rejectivity manifests itself with hatred and destruction.

Erickson's final stage of development is old age. This stage ranges from the ages of 60 to death. Old age should not be associated with a loss of generativity as the elderly remain creatively productive. The elderly can be caring grandparents and remain caring members of society. Old age is a time of joy but also a time of senility. Generalized sensuality is the psychosexual mode of old age and the psychosocial crisis is integrity versus despair with the basic strength of wisdom. The final psychosexual stage generalized sensuality means taking pleasure in different physical sensations such as sight, sound, taste, and smell. Men become more nurturing within nonsexual relationships and women take a greater interest in world affairs (Erikson, Erikson, & Kivnick, 1986). A generalized sensual attitude is dependent on the ability to maintain integrity in the face of despair. The final identity crisis is identity versus despair. People of strong ego identity who learn intimacy and care for people should achieve the syntonic element of integrity. Integrity is an ability to hold together one's sense of self despite diminishing capacities. When people are losing friends, spouses, and physical health, ego integrity may become difficult to maintain. These pressures result in despair expressed with depression or any other attitude indicating disdain of life's boundaries. Despair is an absence of hope giving life little to no meaning. Psychological maturity is dependent on some degree of despair. The struggle between the syntonic and dystonic elements of integrity versus despair produces the basic strength wisdom. Erikson defines wisdom as a disattachment of concern toward life in the face of death. Mature wisdom involves a maintenance of integrity despite cognitive and physical deficits. Wisdom contributes to knowledge passed from generation to generation (Erikson, Erikson, & Kivnick, 1986). The core of pathology during old age is disdain which is a reaction to the feelings of helplessness. Rejectivity during adulthood can continue into old age transforming into disdain (Erikson, 1982). Erikson's wife begins putting together a ninth stage of life as herself and her husband Erik age. The ninth stage is a time of very old age when generative abilities are robbed and reduced to no more than waiting for death to occur. Joan's interest in this ninth stage peak while watching her own husband's health decline during the last few years of his life. Unfortunately, Joan too passes away before completing the ninth stage.

References

Erikson, E. H. (1963). *Childhood and society* (2nd ed.). New York: Norton.

Erikson, E. H. (1968). *Identity: Youth and crisis*. New York: Norton.

Erikson, E. H. (1982). *The life cycle completed: A review*. New York: Norton.

Erikson, E. H., Erikson, J. M., & Kivnick, H. Q. (1986). *Vital involvement in old age*. New York: Norton.

Friedman, L. J. (1999). *Identity's architect: A biography of Erik H. Erikson*. New York: Scribner.

Index